Mit Wörterbuch und Vokabelhilfe

Milena Baisch

Englisch lernen mit den Leselöwen
Freundschaftsgeschichten

Aus dem Deutschen übersetzt von David Ingram

Zeichnungen von Dorothea Tust

Loewe

Bibliografische Information Der Deutschen Bibliothek
Die Deutsche Bibliothek verzeichnet diese Publikation in der Deutschen Nationalbibliografie; detaillierte bibliografische Daten sind im Internet über *http://dnb.ddb.de* abrufbar.

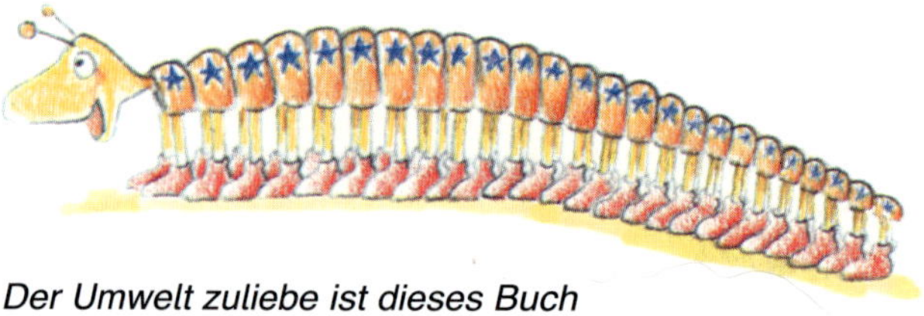

Der Umwelt zuliebe ist dieses Buch auf chlorfrei gebleichtem Papier gedruckt.

ISBN 3-7855-4791-9 – 1. Auflage 2003

Die deutsche Originalausgabe erschien 1997 im Loewe Verlag unter dem Titel „Leselöwen-Freundschaftsgeschichten“
Aus dem Deutschen übersetzt von David Ingram
Umschlagillustration: Dorothea Tust
Umschlaggestaltung: Andreas Henze
Gesamtherstellung: sachsendruck, Plauen
Printed in Germany

www.loewe-verlag.de

Contents

The millepede 11
Cinderella 20
Tom and the traffic jam 28
Dear Paula 38
The cleaning party 46
The oath 54

Liebe Eltern,

unaufhaltsam hält die englische Sprache Einzug in den kindlichen Wortschatz. Was die Sprachwissenschaft nüchtern als Anglizismen betitelt, finden die Kinder überaus spannend. Mit ungebremstem Wissensdurst machen sie sich daran, erste Worte oder Sätze in einer Fremdsprache zu erlernen und zu kommunizieren.

Kinder sind relativ früh mit dem Englischen vertraut, spätestens seit der Einführung des Englischunterrichts an den Grundschulen. Eine Fremdsprache spielerisch, ohne Erfolgszwang, dafür aber mit schnellen Erfolgserlebnissen lernen, so lautet das Motto.
Dieses Prinzip haben wir auch den Englisch-Ausgaben unserer Erstlese-Reihe *Leselöwen* zu Grunde gelegt. In abgeschlossenen Geschichten können die kindlichen Leser ihre ersten Englischkenntnisse anwenden und vertiefen. Die Sprache ist einfach gehalten, die wichtigsten Vokabeln sind im Text markiert und werden in ihrer konkreten Bedeutung am Rand auf Deutsch erklärt. Verben werden dabei gleich in der jeweiligen Person, Adjektive in der flektierten

Form übersetzt. Der Sinn eines Satzes lässt sich so schnell und ohne lästiges Nachschlagen erschließen. Viele Begriffe werden zusätzlich in den Illustrationen durch Wort-Bild-Zuweisungen erläutert.
Im Anhang finden sich sowohl die wichtigsten Vokabeln aus dem Text in alphabetischer Reihenfolge als auch ein speziell dem jeweiligen Thema zu Grunde gelegter Wortschatz auf einer praktischen Ausklappseite.
Die Verben stehen hier im Infinitiv, da an dieser Stelle der Hauptakzent eher auf der Erweiterung des Wortschatzes als auf der Erschließung eines Wortes innerhalb eines Satzes liegt. Dabei werden nicht alle möglichen Bedeutungen im Deutschen angegeben, sondern nur die wichtigsten.
Und wenn Sie mit Ihrem Kind gleichzeitig auch das Hörverständnis und die Sprechfertigkeit trainieren möchten, sind bei Jumbo zu jedem englischen *Leselöwen*-Band die entsprechenden Hörkassetten erhältlich.

Ihren Kindern viel Spaß und Erfolg mit
„Englisch lernen mit den Leselöwen“
wünscht Ihnen Ihr

Leselöwen-Englisch-Team

The millepede

Felix kicks his new football around. He looks at the children from Mill Street. Silke, Frank, Petra, Larus and Tobias all draw very fast.

"Have you got red chalk?" Frank asks. He wants to draw a wild dragon monster.

Silke gives Frank the chalk. "Give it back soon, I want to draw the mushrooms."

Felix watches the children every afternoon. They draw a jungle with all sorts of things in it: purple and yellow palm trees, green spotted tigers, and even a giraffe with wings! Lara and Tobias draw a millepede. It's a caterpillar with one thousand legs. But they can't draw a thousand legs, so it only has fifty legs.

kickt

Kreide

Drachen

Pilze

Dschungel

Palmen

gepunktete

Flügeln

Tausendfüßler; Raupe

Tobias wants to draw a blue star on the back of the millepede. Then Tobias sees two shoes. They are in the way. The two shoes belong to Felix.

Rücken

sind im Weg

"Hey, Felix! Are you crazy?" Tobias shouts. "Get off my millepede!"

Felix turns round and runs away. He runs all the way home. He goes into his bedroom and slams the door.

Geh herunter von

schlägt zu

After a while, Dad comes in. "Why don't you go out and play with the other children?" he asks.

Felix just says: "I don't want to."

Dad says: "Then invite someone here! You've got your computer games."

That is a good idea. The new computer games are really good. But the games are for two players. When he plays alone, Felix can't pass the first level. Felix is angry now, because he can't play alone.

Nach einer Weile

lade ein

wirklich

Stufe; wütend

allein

Felix remembers the stupid millepede. The other children just don't want to play with him!

Suddenly Felix gets up and picks up his big water pistol. "I'll show them!" he says. Felix goes to the tap and fills the water pistol with water. All the way to the top. Then he goes to Mill Street.

erinnert sich an

blöden

Plötzlich

hebt auf; Wasserspritzpistole

Denen werde ich es zeigen!

Wasserhahn

Petra, Lara, Tobias, Silke and Frank are still in their jungle. Felix hides behind a car and watches them. Lara and Tobias only need to draw three more legs on the millepede.

"Oh dear!" Tobias says. "The leg is far too long!"

"Oh no, Tobias!" Lara says. "Now we've got forty-nine short legs and a long one. That looks really stupid!"

versteckt sich

müssen

Beine

viel zu lang

kurze

wirklich blöd

Silke and Petra leave their mushroom drawings and look at Tobias.

"How can he walk along?" Petra asks.

"Well, I suppose he has to limp!" Silke says.

Tobias is very sad. He wants to cry. "I want a nice millepede. And now my millepede has one wrong leg!"

Zeichnungen

nehme an

hinken

weinen

Felix wonders what to do, too. Then he suddenly remembers the water pistol. He aims it at the millepede's long leg.

"Hey, who's that?" the children shout. "We're all wet!"

Felix comes out from behind the car. Now there is a small puddle of water over the millepede's long leg.

fragt sich

plötzlich

erinnert sich an

zielt

nass

Pfütze

"The leg is gone!" Tobias shouts. He is very shocked.
Felix takes a piece of chalk and draws a new leg. It looks good, and it is not too long.
"There you are," Felix says. "Now your millepede is all right again."
Petra looks at Felix. "Please squirt your water pistol at my mushroom, Felix."
"Of course," Felix says. Suddenly the mushroom is gone.
Petra draws the mushroom again. It looks better now.

weg

geschockt

ein Stück von

Tausendfüßler; in Ordnung

spritze

Pilz

Natürlich

Plötzlich

Then Frank shouts to Felix. "Hey! The coconuts look really stupid. Can you fire the pistol at them, please?"

Kokosnüsse
wirklich blöd; schießen

"No problem," Felix says. He squirts his water pistol at all the bad drawings.

spritzt

In the evening the children put away their chalk. "Can you come tomorrow, Felix?" Tobias asks.

morgen

"Oh yes!" Felix says. Then he takes his water pistol home.

Cinderella

Meike and Katja are in the school playground. "That's not fair! That's not fair at all!" Meike stamps her foot on the ground. "Sina is not my friend anymore!" Katja agrees with her.

Schulhof
gerecht
stampft
nicht mehr
stimmt ihr zu

The school play this year is "Cinderella". The teacher wants Sina to play Cinderella. And she wants Meike and Katja to play the ugly sisters. Meike and Katja want to play Cinderella as well. But instead, the teacher wants Sina to play the part. Meike and Katja are very angry.

ugly sisters – *böse Schwestern*
as well – *auch*
instead – *stattdessen*
angry – *wütend*

"Sina doesn't care about you!" Katja says.

"No, she doesn't," Meike says. "I think she is very selfish."

care about – *kümmert sich um*
selfish – *selbstsüchtig*

The bell rings for the next lesson. Every day Sina and Meike usually hold hands. But today Meike holds hands with Katja.

Two weeks go by. Sina and Meike never look at each other. They do not sit together in the classroom any more. They do not do their homework together. And at the weekend, Meike goes to visit Katja instead of Sina.

Schulglocke
Schulstunde
halten sich an den Händen
vergehen
sich ansehen
sitzen nicht mehr nebeneinander
besuchen
anstelle von

Today is the day of the school play. Everyone is very nervous. The play begins at three o'clock in the afternoon.

Suddenly the teacher comes into the classroom. She has the costumes in her arms. She is very nervous. "Listen, children. We have a problem," she says.

aufgeregt

Plötzlich

Kostüme

"Sina is sick and she can't do the play."

The children all murmur.

The teacher says: "I have an idea. Meike, perhaps you can be Cinderella instead of Sina. Then Manuela can be the second ugly sister."

Manuela agrees to the idea. Meike agrees as well but she is not really happy. She is sorry for Sina. Poor Sina has to stay at home and cannot be in the play.

But now, Meike must learn Sina's part. And very quickly, too.

The play is a big success. Meike is a very good Cinderella. The people clap very loudly. Meike bows to them. She is very popular. Everyone thinks she is great.

krank
murmeln vor sich hin
vielleicht
anstelle von
böse Schwester
ist einverstanden mit
auch
wirklich
Ihr tut Leid; Arme
Teil
Erfolg
klatschen
verbeugt sich
beliebt
großartig

Then Meike sees Sina's parents in the audience. Meike asks them: "Is Sina all right?"

"Sina is very sad that she cannot be here," Sina's mother says. "Can you visit her? I think she wants you to do that."

Publikum

in Ordnung

besuchen

möchte, dass du das machst

Meike goes with Sina's parents. Sina is in the bedroom. "Hello," Meike whispers.

Sina says quietly: "Hello, Meike."

Meike feels nervous. Then she says to Sina: "I think you are a better Cinderella than me."

whispers: *flüstert*

quietly: *leise*

nervous: *aufgeregt*

Then Sina asks Meike:
"Are you still angry with me?"
Meike shakes her head.
"And what about you?"
Sina shakes her head, too.
Then the two girls start to laugh. Meike takes off her shoes. She gets into Sina's bed and says: "I want to stay here until you are better!"

böse mit mir

schüttelt den Kopf

zieht aus

bleiben

bis

Tom and the traffic jam

Tom and his parents are in a big traffic jam. The radio says: "There is a thirty-mile queue on the A 20 ..." Tom's father switches off the radio and asks: "Why does this always happen to us?!" He is annoyed because the car is stuck in the traffic jam. But Tom thinks that traffic jams are not so bad after all.

traffic jam – *Verkehrsstau*
thirty-mile queue – *dreißig-Kilometer-Schlange*
switches off – *schaltet aus*
happen – *passiert*
is annoyed – *ärgert sich*
is stuck – *steckt (fest)*
after all – *schließlich*

He likes to look out of the window at the people in the other cars. A red car overtakes them now on the left. In the back seat is a little girl. She reads a Mickey Mouse comic. Tom rolls down the window and shows her his comic. It's a Mickey Mouse comic, too! The girl smiles at Tom. But then the cars start to move and the red car disappears again.

überholt

Rücksitz

kurbelt herunter

lächelt

bewegen

verschwindet

"I think you'd better read your comics again," Tom's mother says. "This is a very big traffic jam."

du solltest lieber

Verkehrsstau

That is the last thing Tom wants to do. He knows all his Mickey Mouse comics by heart. Numbers 176 to 181. Then Tom has an idea. Perhaps the little girl in the red car has a new comic?

das Letzte

auswendig

Die Nummern

Vielleicht

The cars are still in the jam. Some people get out and start to walk around and stretch their legs. Tom is tired, too.

"See you later!" he says to his parents and he gets out of the car! The line of cars

steigen aus

vertreten sich die Beine

müde

Bis später

Schlange

stretches as far as his eyes can see. Big ones, small ones, colourful ones, grey ones … Tom stands on tiptoe. Then he sees the car he wants: the red one with the bikes on the roof! Before his mother can speak, Tom quickly takes his comics. He walks down to the red car. It is not very far away. The girl is there beside the car!

zieht sich

stellt sich auf die Zehenspitzen

weit weg

neben

"There you are!" she says. — *Hier bist du!*

Tom nods. "Yes. Excuse me, but do you want to swap comics?" — *nickt*; *tauschen*

"Oh, number 179!" the girl says happily. "I don't have that one. What do you want for it?"

Tom is not sure. Then someone suddenly shouts: "Klara! Get back in!" Tom looks round. Further along the queue, the cars start to move. — *sicher*; *plötzlich*; *Weiter vorn; Schlange*; *bewegen*

"I must go back," the girl says.

Tom must go back, too.
But how? Suddenly he is
all alone beside the cars.
Then he hears the girl shout:
"You can't get back again!
Get into our car!"
Tom has no time to think. He
jumps into the red car. Then
the cars all start to move.

Plötzlich
ganz allein
neben
springt
bewegen

"Well, well, who have we here?" the girl's mother says. She is surprised.

"I'm Tom but I have to get back to my parents," Tom says. There's a tear in his eye.

"Don't cry," the girl says. She puts her arm round him. "I'm Klara. And I have an idea."

wen haben wir denn da

überrascht

Träne

weine

First they wait until Tom's parents drive past. Then they bang on the car window.

Tom's parents see Tom in the car. Now they are very happy. They drive beside the red car. Then Klara writes on a piece of paper. She gives it to Tom. "Hold it up to the window," she says. "Then your parents can see it."

vorbeifahren

schlagen

neben

Stück Papier

Halte es hoch

Tom looks at the piece of paper. It says *Next Services*. What a brilliant idea!

Stück Papier
Nächste Raststätte
glänzende

Tom is soon back with his parents. Before they leave, Tom whispers to Klara. Then they swap their addresses and their comics.

zurück bei
flüstert
tauschen

Tom's mother asks: "Who is that girl, Tom?"

Tom says: "That is my girlfriend Klara."

Dear Paula

Marie looks out of her window. A bird family is in the apple tree. Marie is sad because she has to move to a new flat. Now she cannot see the bird family again.

Vogelfamilie

umziehen

Wohnung

"Moving house is really stupid!" Marie says. She looks at the birds: "Why can't I stay here and watch you? You've got such a lovely nest." Marie sighs. She is so unhappy.

umziehen

wirklich blöd

so ein

seufzt; unglücklich

Suddenly she hears someone call out to her: "Yoo hoo! Marie!" Marie looks down. Her father wants her to come down to the removal lorry.

Marie goes down and sees two grown-ups and a girl. "These are the Schuberts," her mother says. "Paula Schubert is in her third year at school, just like you."

Paula grins at Marie.

Plötzlich

zurufen

Umzugswagen

Erwachsene

grinst

"Do you want to see my hamster, Paula?" Marie asks.

"Ooh yes!" Paula says.

The two girls go upstairs to Marie's room. It looks very empty. The walls are bare. The room is full of boxes. In the middle of the room there is Pfiffi in the hamster's cage.

leer; nackt

Mitten in

"Can I take him on my arm?" Paula asks. "I've got a hamster, too."

Marie nods. "Yes, of course."

Paula picks up Pfiffi and strokes him. The hamster is very happy and comfortable.

"Why don't you move into my room?" Marie says. "Then a hamster can be here again!"

Paula nods. "Yes! And we can put the cage in the same place as Pfiffi's cage!"

nickt; natürlich

hebt auf

streichelt

behaglich

umziehen

lift

The new flat is very different. It is in a skyscraper with twenty-three floors. Marie takes the lift four times a day. She feels lonely, and so she sometimes takes Pfiffi with her.

"Look for some friends to play with," her mother says.

"No one is interested," Marie says. "The boys only want to play football, and they all laugh at me because I am a girl. That's why I'm worried."

Wohnung; anders
Wolkenkratzer
Stockwerken
Aufzug
einsam
besorgt

Marie's mother is surprised. "But what about the girls?" she asks.

"They play silly games all the time and they giggle. I think they're stupid. They don't want to play with me either. And perhaps they giggle at me."

überrascht
was ist mit
kichern
blöd
auch nicht;
vielleicht

Marie's mother pats her on the head. "Don't worry, Marie. You'll find some friends."

But Marie knows that only one friend is really interested in her: Pfiffi! She takes him out

tätschelt
Mach dir keine Sorgen
wirklich

of his cage. "Come on, Pfiffi
I have a really good idea.
I want to write a letter. A letter
to Paula in our old house!"

Marie quickly takes out some
paper and a pen and writes:

really: wirklich

Dear Paula,

How are you? I'm bored. I like the new flat. But I don't know any children yet. We live on the eighth floor and we have a lift. If you are hungry, go to the kiosk on the corner. The sweets are really good!

Yours, Marie

PS: Can you write back to me?

I'm bored: Ich langweile mich.
don't … yet: noch nicht
lift: Aufzug; hungry: hungrig
corner: Ecke; sweets: Süßigkeiten
really: wirklich

Marie puts the letter in an envelope. Then she takes it to the letterbox. Four days later she gets a letter from Paula! Marie jumps for joy! She opens it and reads:

Umschlag
Briefkasten; später
springt vor Freude (in die Luft)

Dear Marie,

Thank you for your letter. I'm bored, too. Why aren't we pen friends? Then we can send lots of letters to each other! There's a bird's nest near my window. I watch it every day. One of the baby birds can fly!

Yours, Paula

Ich langweile mich auch.
Brieffreunde
einander
Vogelnest

The cleaning party

Jonas looks for his key. He wants to go home quickly because today is "Mrs Kugelschmitt Day." Mrs Kugelschmitt is the cleaning lady. Once a week she cleans the flat for Jonas and his parents.

Jonas unlocks the front door. "Yoo hoo!" he shouts and throws his satchel in a corner. Mrs Kugelschmitt is there.

"Good afternoon, dear lady!" Jonas says. "May I kiss your hand?" He always talks in a funny way to Mrs Kugelschmitt. They have a secret language. Mrs Kugelschmitt is quite old. She knows how to talk politely.

But today she does not answer.

Schlüssel

Putzfrau

Einmal in der Woche

Wohnung

schließt auf

Schulranzen; Ecke

Darf ich Ihre Hand küssen?

auf eine lustige Art

Geheimsprache

ziemlich

höflich

She just turns round and goes into the kitchen. Jonas can smell the food! "Oh, dumplings! How very kind of you, dear lady!" But Mrs Kugelschmitt still says nothing. Then Jonas notices that she has tears in her eyes.

"Oh, Jonas," she sighs. "It's my little canary."

riechen
Klöße
bemerkt
Tränen
seufzt
Kanarienvogel

Mrs Kugelschmitt has a little canary with yellow feathers in a cage. "My little canary is dead!"

Kanarienvogel
Federn
tot

Jonas doesn't know what to say. "May I lay the table, Your Majesty?" he asks. He wants her to be happy.

When Jonas has lunch with Mrs Kugelschmitt, it is different. Jonas always has his lunch under the table. That is because the chairs are on top of it. Mrs Kugelschmitt always does that, so that she can clean better.

den Tisch decken
anders
darauf

Jonas takes the tablecloth and puts it over the chairs. Then they have a nice cave under the table. Then Jonas lays the table. Jonas looks at the kitchen. "You can bring the dumplings now, dear lady!" he calls.

Tischtuch

Höhle

deckt den Tisch

Klöße

Mrs Kugelschmitt arrives with the steaming pot. She sniffs a little. "Do be seated, madam!" Jonas says. It is a bit difficult for Mrs Kugelschmitt to sit down. She is rather fat and finds it hard to fit under the table!

Then the two of them start to eat the delicious dumplings.

dampfenden Topf
schnieft ein bisschen
Nehmen Sie Platz
ein bisschen schwierig
ziemlich; findet es schwierig zu passen
köstlichen Klöße

"Cook, I must say your dumplings are quite delicious," Jonas says.

Mrs Kugelschmitt smiles at last.

After the meal Jonas wipes his mouth with his napkin. "Okay," he says. "Now it's time for a cleaning party!"

Mrs Kugelschmitt looks a bit unhappy. "Oh Jonas, I don't feel like a party," she says.

But Jonas turns on the radio very loudly. When he cleans the house with Mrs Kugelschmitt, they do it differently from most people. Jonas holds the duster like a microphone. When somebody sings on the radio, Jonas sings as well. He pretends that he is the singer. "One, two, three, four!" Jonas likes rock music. The louder it is, the faster he cleans.

ich muss sagen
Klöße;
ganz köstlich
endlich
wischt ab
Serviette
Putzparty
ein bisschen unglücklich
Lust haben auf
schaltet ein
anders als
Staubtuch
auch
tut so, als ob
lauter
schneller

Mrs Kugelschmitt cleans the kitchen floor. She likes cleaning parties but today she is very quiet.

"Oh no!" Jonas suddenly cries. "Folk music!"

The man on the radio plays a piece of folk music. Jonas hates folk music. He switches off the radio. Then he hears a voice from the kitchen: Mrs Kugelschmitt is singing!

Küchenboden
ruhig
schreit plötzlich
Volksmusik!
Stück
schaltet aus
Stimme
singt

Jonas goes to her and looks at her in astonishment. — *erstaunt*
"You're not sad anymore!" — *nicht mehr*

Mrs Kugelschmitt laughs. "Put on the music again! — *mach an*
That lovely tune!" — *schöne Melodie*

Jonas runs to the radio. The two of them sing and clean all afternoon. Jonas decides to — *beschließt*
do the washing-up. — *Abwasch*

Then his parents come home.

"How do you do it, Mrs Kugelschmitt?" his mother asks. "Jonas never does the washing-up normally!" — *normalerweise*

Then Mrs Kugelschmitt and Jonas laugh and wink at each other. — *zwinkern einander zu*

The oath

"Let's go!" Nina shouts. She puts on her inline skates and holds on to the carrier at the back of Olli's bicycle. Then they both race downhill.

"Look out, here comes a bump!" Olli calls.

"Don't go so fast, Olli!" Nina shouts. When they go uphill Nina lets go.

hält sich fest an; Gepäckträger

rasen bergab

Pass auf

Unebenheit

bergauf

lässt los

Today they are in the park. Sometimes a dog gets in the way. Suddenly Olli stops!

"Hey, what's the matter?" Nina asks.

"I'm bored," Olli says. "I only pedal and you have all the fun."

"You're right," Nina says. Then she has an idea. "I know what. Why don't we do a swap?"

Hund kreuzt ihren Weg

Plötzlich

was ist los?

Ich langweile mich

trete in die Pedalen

Du hast Recht

Ich weiß was.

tauschen

Nina sits down and takes off her inline skates. Olli puts down the bicycle and takes off his shoes. Then they swap.

Nina decides to try the bike. She does a practice round and nearly falls down. Her legs are too short and she has to stand on tiptoe.
"Stupid bike," she says.

"It's not stupid at all," Olli says. "Your legs are too short, that's all." He stands up on the skates. Then he waves his arms wildly and lands on his bottom!

"Stupid skates!" he says.

"I beg your pardon?" Nina asks. "They're not stupid at all. You just can't skate properly, that's your problem!
Your feet are much
too big!"

zieht aus

tauschen

beschließt

Proberunde

beinahe

auf Zehenspitzen stehen

Blödes

überhaupt nicht

das ist alles

rudert

wild; landet

Hosenboden

Wie bitte?

richtig (Inline-skates) fahren

This is too much for Olli. He sits down and takes off the inline skates again. “Get off my bike right now! I’m the only person who can ride it!”

“There you are,” Nina says. But she doesn’t put the bike on its stand. She just lets it fall over.

zieht aus

Geh herunter

augenblicklich; der Einzige

Da hast du es

stellt das Fahrrad auf den Fahrradständer

lässt es umfallen

Olli and Nina are very angry with each other. Olli goes home in one direction and Nina goes home in the other. They don't even say goodbye.

wütend
aufeinander
Richtung
andere

The next day Nina does her homework. Maths is easy for her but she has trouble with the essay. The title is "My biggest wish". Nina and Olli usually do their homework

Mathematik
hat Schwierigkeiten mit
Aufsatz
Mein größter Wunsch

together. Olli often has really good ideas for the essays.

Today Olli isn't there and Nina just can't do her homework. Then the phone rings.

It's Olli. "I can't do maths," he says. "Can you help me?"

Nina thinks about it and then she says: "But only if you tell me what to write for the essay."

"Okay," Olli says. "Let's meet at the secret hideout in half an hour!"

Nina immediately puts on her inline skates and goes to the park. The hideout is inside a big bush.

When Nina arrives Olli is already there. "Now I'll tell you my biggest wish," he says. "Let's swear an oath never to argue again!"

wirklich
Aufsätze
Telefon klingelt
Mathematik
denkt nach
nur wenn
Geheimversteck
sofort
Versteck; inmitten
großen Busches
schwören; Eid
sich streiten

Nina thinks it is a good idea. "Yes, let's swear an oath as friends!" she says. The two of them sit down opposite each other and look in each others eyes.

schwören; Eid

einander gegenüber

sehen sich einander in die Augen

Nina raises her right hand slowly. "I swear that Olli is my very best friend."

hebt

langsam; schwöre

Olli waits a moment and then he does the same. And then he says: "Now we have to kiss each other."

macht dasselbe

küssen

Nina is a bit confused. But she pouts her lips.

Olli and Nina move their faces closer and closer together. So close that their lips touch.

It feels funny. Warm and soft. They don't know if it lasts for two minutes or for half an hour. But finally they move their lips apart and Nina takes a deep breath.

"Okay," she says. "It's decided. We are now the best of friends for ever."

Olli nods. "For ever and ever."

durcheinander
spitzt ihre Lippen
bewegen
Gesichter immer näher zueinander
Lippen (sich) berühren
fühlt sich komisch an
weich
dauert
schließlich
auseinander
holt tief Luft
Es ist entschieden
für immer
nickt

Dein Wörterbuch A–I

A	after	nach
	after all	schließlich
	after a while	nach einer Weile
	all right	in Ordnung
	alone	allein
	apart	auseinander
	to arrive	ankommen
	as well	auch
B	beside	neben
	bird	Vogel
C	to call out	ausrufen
	to care	sich kümmern, sorgen, Acht geben
	to cry	weinen, schreien
D	to decide	beschließen, sich entscheiden
	different	anders
	difficult	schwierig
	to disappear	verschwinden
E	each other	einander
	empty	leer

F	far away	weit weg
	far too	viel zu
	faster	schneller
	to feel	fühlen, sich anfühlen, empfinden
	finally	schließlich
	for ever	für immer
	funny	komisch, lustig
G	to get off	herunter-, ab-, aussteigen, davonkommen
	to get out	aussteigen, herausbringen
	to giggle	kichern
	gone	weg, vergangen, vorbei
	great	großartig, prima, groß, gewaltig
	to grin	grinsen
H	to happen	passieren
	to hide	sich verstecken
I	I beg your pardon?	Wie bitte?
	immediately	sofort

Dein Wörterbuch I–Q

I	inside	inmitten, in
	instead	stattdessen
	to invite	einladen
J	to jump	springen
	just	genau, gerade (noch), bloß
K	key	Schlüssel
	to kick	kicken, treten, strampeln
L	last	letzte
	to last	dauern
	later	später
	legs	Beine
	lonely	einsam
	long	lang
M	to move	bewegen, transportieren, umziehen
N	nearly	beinahe
	nervous	aufgeregt
	normally	normalerweise
	not anymore	nicht mehr

	not either	auch nicht
	not yet	noch nicht
O	oath	Eid
	of course	selbstverständlich
	only if	nur wenn
	only person	Einzige
	opposite each other	einander gegenüber
	other	andere
P	paper	Papier
	part	Teil
	perhaps	vielleicht
	phone	Telefon
	to pick up	aufheben
	piece	Stück
	poor	arm, bedauernswert
	to pretend	vorgeben, so tun, als ob
	properly	richtig
Q	quite	ziemlich, ganz, völlig
	quietly	leise

R	to raise	heben, aufheben, hochheben
	rather	ziemlich
	really	wirklich, echt
	to remember	sich erinnern
	right now	augenblicklich
	to ring	klingeln
S	see you later	bis später
	short	kurz
	sick	krank
	slowly	langsam
	to smell	riechen
	to stay	bleiben
	stupid	dumm
	success	Erfolg
	such a	so ein
	suddenly	plötzlich
	to suppose	annehmen, sich vorstellen, voraussetzen
	sure	sicher
	to switch off	ausschalten, abschalten